# 'Abdu'l-Bahá's

## Little Brown Cat

Tatterdemalion Blue

First Published by Tatterdemalion Blue in 2021

Words © Carolyn Sparey Fox 2021
Illustrations © Alan McKay 2021

A CIP catalogue record for this book is available from the British Library

Cover design and layout by Tatterdemalion Blue

ISBN 978-1-915123-04-6

Tatterdemalion Blue
74 Maxwell Place
Stirling
FK8 1JU

www.tatterdemalionblue.com

# 'Abdu'l-Bahá's

## Little Brown Cat

Written by
### Carolyn Sparey Fox

Illustrated by
### Alan McKay

# Dedication

'Abdu'l-Bahá's Little Brown Cat was written for
children in commemoration of the centenary of
the passing of 'Abdu'l-Bahá in November 1921.

# Introduction

This is a story for children of all ages, and for adults who like to read to them. All people and events in the story are historical, verified with relevant references and sources. It's clear from contemporary records that 'Abdu'l-Bahá had a brown cat at this time, the only fiction in the story being the suggestion that His cat was often on hand to observe what was taking place. What the cat does and thinks are the only fiction in the story.

The illustration of the Shrine of the Báb shows the building as it was in the time of 'Abdu'l-Bahá, with a faint suggestion of the magnificent superstructure which was to come later, in fulfilment of 'Abdu'l-Bahá's wish.

'Abdu'l-Bahá was the eldest son of Bahá'u'lláh, founder of the Bahá'í Faith, and Bahá'u'lláh appointed 'Abdu'l-Bahá to be His successor after He passed away in 1892.

'Abdu'l-Bahá is referred to as the Centre of the Covenant, the perfect example of Bahá'u'lláh's teachings and Interpreter of His Word. He was born in 1844, and was with Bahá'u'lláh during all four of His exiles, eventually arriving at the prison city of 'Akká, in Palestine, in 1868.[1]

Following several years of extreme hardship, Bahá'u'lláh was able to move out of 'Akká to a mansion in the nearby countryside, and it was there that He passed away in May 1892.

When 'Abdu'l-Bahá moved from 'Akká to Haifa in August 1910, He and His family lived in a beautiful house which He had built at the bottom of Haparsim Street, just a little distance from the harbour.[2] And not very far from Haparsim Street, half way up the steep slopes of Mount Carmel, stood the Shrine of the Báb,[3] looking out over the town and the Mediterranean Sea.

During the final two years of His life, 'Abdu'l-Bahá had a cat,[4] and although nothing is known about her other than she was brown, a couple of reliable sources suggest that 'Abdu'l-Bahá was very fond of her.

This book tells the story of 'Abdu'l-Bahá's last years through the eyes and ears of His little brown cat; all facts concerning 'Abdu'l-Bahá, Shoghi Effendi, and the people who either lived in Haifa or visited, are taken from historic sources (see bibliography).

Carolyn Sparey Fox is a professional musician and author living in Scotland. Little Brown Cat is one of three illustrated stories which Carolyn has written for children.

Alan McKay is an architect, designing houses in the remote and beautiful Shetland Islands. His illustrations of Little Brown Cat were inspired by his family cat, 'Carmen'.

# 'Abdu'l-Bahá's

## Little Brown Cat

Nobody could remember exactly when the little brown cat first arrived in 'Abdu'l-Bahá's garden in Haparsim Street, and since nobody knew what her name was, she was simply known as Little Brown Cat. She had delicate pointed ears, large watchful eyes, and a long tail which waved from side to side as she walked. And because Little Brown Cat loved to be close to 'Abdu'l-Bahá she often sunned herself in His garden, with her head resting on her two front paws.

Several family members and fellow Bahá'ís lived with 'Abdu'l-Bahá in the house at the bottom of Haparsim Street, but Little Brown Cat really only had eyes for 'Abdu'l-Bahá and two others, His wife Munírih, who was known as the Holy Mother, and His sister Bahíyyih, known as the Greatest Holy Leaf.

Little Brown Cat would watch 'Abdu'l-Bahá, the Holy Mother and the Greatest Holy Leaf as they went about their daily business, and when she couldn't see them she would listen out for their kind voices coming from somewhere inside the house.

Although 'Abdu'l-Bahá was an old man He was one of the most lively and joyful people that Little Brown Cat had ever met. Even when He was feeling tired He would ask people if they were happy, and sometimes He would ask them several times if they were happy, as if He needed to be sure that they really were. Little Brown Cat didn't need to be asked if she was happy because 'Abdu'l-Bahá was never very far away, and being near Him made her very happy indeed.

It had been very quiet in Haparsim Street during the Great War, especially when 'Abdu'l-Bahá had decided to protect His family and fellow Bahá'ís by moving them to a little village in the foothills of Galilee.[5]

Although it had been so quiet, 'Abdu'l-Bahá had been busy making sure that the people of Haifa had enough to eat when food was scarce by growing and storing wheat near Lake Galilee. As soon as the war ended visitors started arriving once more, and it was then that Little Brown Cat began to realise that 'Abdu'l-Bahá was a very important person. She also noticed that He began to spend a lot of time with one of His grandsons who had just returned from studying in Beirut; he was called Shoghi Effendi, and he was so kind, gentle and wise that Little Brown Cat soon loved being near him almost as much as with 'Abdu'l-Bahá.

Because Little Brown Cat didn't want to miss anything she tried very hard to stay awake during the day, and to be close by when visitors arrived; she learned to be extremely observant, and sometimes when she looked as if she was sleeping she was actually listening to everything going on around her. Every morning at dawn the sound of bagpipes rang out over the town from the British military headquarters as people began to stir, and Little Brown Cat stretched herself from head to toe, in preparation for the new day.[6]

As the months passed so many people came to visit 'Abdu'l-Bahá that there were times when Little Brown Cat couldn't remember who was arriving and

who was leaving, but she was in no doubt at all that she was a very privileged cat because she had the honour of being close to so many interesting people. There were the people who lived in 'Abdu'l-Bahá's house, and others who lived close by who seemed to come and go almost every day. Then there were the pilgrims, those coming from the east staying in the Eastern Pilgrim House further up the mountain, and those from the west in the Western Pilgrim House, on the other side of Haparsim Street from 'Abdu'l-Bahá's house, which had an impressive iron gate surrounded by beautiful purple bougainvillea.[7]

Some of the western pilgrims sailed across the sea all the way from America, and others came from countries like France, England, Scotland, and Japan. All the pilgrims who visited Haifa came to spend precious time with 'Abdu'l-Bahá, to ask Him questions and listen to His wise words; they also came to say prayers in the Shrine of the Báb, and when there was no moonlight at night Little Brown Cat was comforted to see that a few lamps had been lit in front of the Shrine. Sometimes she wished that she could walk up the steep hill to the Shrine of the Báb, but since it was such a long way to go, she decided to stay where she felt safe, in Haparsim Street.

One of the visitors who travelled from England was Dr. John Esslemont, who brought with him part of an important book he was writing, which 'Abdu'l-Bahá wished to discuss with him.[8]

Little Brown Cat knew that the book was important because Dr. John and 'Abdu'l-Bahá spent many hours talking about it, even though Dr. John suffered from ill health and had to spend time resting in the Pilgrim House.

One November day,[9] a group of people arrived in Haparsim Street after a stormy voyage across the Mediterranean Sea, and as soon as they were taken to the Pilgrim House, Shoghi Effendi welcomed them with a lovely bunch of flowers. When Little Brown Cat set eyes on the new arrivals she had a feeling that life was about to become extremely busy and enjoyable; she was right, for the first person she saw was a very lively and joyful man called Fujita, and as soon as she noticed the kind twinkle in his eyes she knew that they would be good friends.

Fujita was a young Japanese Bahá'í who had travelled with 'Abdu'l-Bahá during His visit to America a few years earlier, and when 'Abdu'l-Bahá invited him to come and serve in His home and take care of the Pilgrims in the Western Pilgrim House in Haifa, Fujita didn't hesitate. And that wasn't all, because Fujita had arrived with a special present from a Bahá'í lady in America; it was a very large, very beautiful, and very shiny motor car which he was to look after and drive from time to time.[10] Little Brown Cat was particularly happy because she was sure that in hot weather the

magnificent car would be the perfect place to shelter away from the sun, unless, of course, Fujita was using it to drive visitors around Haifa.

Little Brown Cat liked Fujita; she liked him very much, especially since he was the person who looked after her and made sure she had enough to eat. And Fujita loved 'Abdu'l-Bahá very much. During quiet early mornings, before the day really started, they often drank tea or had breakfast together, and one day during lunch 'Abdu'l-Bahá asked Fujita to show Him how to eat rice with chopsticks, which caused much merriment to everyone gathered at the table. Often Little Brown Cat heard them laughing, especially when 'Abdu'l-Bahá asked Fujita to grow a beard, because even when it had been growing for a long long time it was never any more than a few very straggly thin hairs; and when 'Abdu'l-Bahá leaned over to stroke it they would both laugh and laugh and laugh.

Among Fujita's fellow travellers to Haifa was a young girl called Margaret, and Little Brown Cat took to her the moment she saw her arriving with her parents at the Western Pilgrim House in Haparsim Street.[11] It rained and rained during their visit to Haifa, and since Little Brown Cat didn't like rain, she didn't really want to sit in 'Abdu'l-Bahá's garden or outside the Western Pilgrim House. Instead, she sought shelter under the trailing bougainvillea leaves, or under the steps leading up to the front of the Western Pilgrim House, because more than anything else she wanted to stay dry.

Little Brown Cat soon realised that as long as she stayed awake and alert in her shelter under the steps she was able to see quite a lot that was happening. She noticed that Margaret didn't like to be woken so early in the mornings when the bagpipes sounded nearby, and later on she could see 'Abdu'l-Bahá arriving to share lunch with the pilgrims; often He came carrying jasmine blossoms from near the Shrine of the Báb, sprinkling them over the tablecloth and filling the air with their sweet scent. Sometimes when the food was brought across from 'Abdu'l-Bahá's house Little Brown Cat could tell that there was fish on the menu, because the smell was so tempting she could hardly stop herself from reaching out a paw.

One day Little Brown Cat noticed that Margaret looked so happy that her face shone. It was the day that 'Abdu'l-Bahá gave her a new name, the same name as His sister, the Greatest Holy Leaf, whose name was Bahíyyih, meaning 'full of light'. Margaret loved the name that 'Abdu'l-Bahá gave her so much that she was known as Bahíyyih from that day onwards. Bahíyyih's days in Haifa were filled with joy despite the rain, for being with 'Abdu'l-Bahá was just like being in the sunshine.

Everyone who met 'Abdu'l-Bahá knew that He was the kindest person they had ever met, and one day Bahíyyih witnessed that His kindness included people that He didn't know. Bahíyyih's father had brought with him to Haifa some beautiful soft wool cloth especially for 'Abdu'l-Bahá, and when it was shown to the Greatest Holy Leaf, she asked 'Abdu'l-Bahá if she could have it made into a loose cloak.[12]

Although 'Abdu'l-Bahá told her that He didn't need another cloak, the Greatest Holy Leaf persuaded Him to accept out of politeness, and soon afterwards Bahíyyih and her parents were happy to see Him wearing a lovely new cloak. However, the very next day as they looked out into Haparsim Street, they were surprised to see a poor beggar walking by wearing the very same cloak. Although Little Brown Cat had been looking forward to sitting on the lovely soft woollen cloak, she was quite happy that 'Abdu'l-Bahá had given it away to someone who needed it far more than she did.

Little Brown Cat was very sad when the time came for Bahíyyih and her parents to leave Haifa.[13] It was raining as they left Haparsim Street for the harbour with Fujita and Shoghi Effendi, and if they had looked very carefully they would have noticed two sad eyes looking out at them from under the bougainvillea bush.[14]

As she surveyed life in Haparsim Street Little Brown Cat noticed that 'Abdu'l-Bahá spent a lot of time with Shoghi Effendi. Quite often they spent hours and hours together, and at other times Shoghi Effendi shut himself away with pens, paper and books, because he was busy translating the Writings and Letters of 'Abdu'l-Bahá from Persian into English so that all the Bahá'ís who spoke English could understand His beautiful and important words. Shoghi Effendi also spent time with the pilgrims who visited Haifa, and as Little Brown Cat watched him from her favourite places in Haparsim Street she began to think that although He always looked happy, He also looked very, very tired. 'Abdu'l-Bahá also noticed that Shoghi Effendi was very tired, and when He decided to send him away for a rest near Paris, in France,[15] Little Brown Cat felt sad because she knew she would miss his joyful presence.

After Shoghi Effendi had left Haifa, life in Haparsim Street carried on much as normal, and although 'Abdu'l-Bahá was always busy, He was never too busy to stroke Little Brown Cat as He passed her by; there were even times when He made sure that she had enough food to eat, which made Little Brown Cat so happy that she purred for a long long time after she had finished her food and carefully cleaned her whiskers.[16]

One spring day, just as Little Brown Cat was settling down for a nap in 'Abdu'l-Bahá's garden, a large shiny car stopped outside the gates; it had arrived to take 'Abdu'l-Bahá to the British Governor's residence, where He was to be knighted for having grown and stored wheat during the war, and for making sure that the people living in Haifa and 'Akká had had enough to eat. As Little Brown Cat watched from her sunny corner of the garden, she saw an elegant-looking chauffeur stepping out of the shiny car, and although everyone ran looking for 'Abdu'l-Bahá in all directions, He was nowhere to be found.

When Little Brown Cat finally saw Him, He was standing close to His beloved servant, 'Isfandiyar, who was used to driving 'Abdu'l-Bahá to meetings on

His horse-drawn carriage. 'Abdu'l-Bahá could see that 'Isfandiyar was feeling sad and unwanted, and so He ordered the horse-drawn carriage to be prepared immediately, and 'Isfandiyar felt so happy as he drove 'Abdu'l-Bahá to the Governor's residence.[17]

'Abdu'l-Bahá had a wish, and His wish was to see Mount Carmel covered in light. And He wanted there to be light shining from inside the Shrine of the Báb, right across the Bay of Haifa to the Shrine of Bahá'u'lláh at Bahjí. Little Brown Cat knew that if such a thing could happen, 'Abdu'l-Bahá would be very happy, as well as all the pilgrims who liked to be able to see as they walked up the mountain to the Shrine of the Báb. Although Little Brown Cat thought that 'Abdu'l-Bahá's wish was an impossible dream, she soon

14

discovered that some dreams come true. And this is how it began to happen.

There was a Bahá'í living in America who was very sad when he heard that the Báb had been in prison with not even a candle for light. His name was Roy Wilhelm,[18] and he decided to write to 'Abdu'l-Bahá, asking if he could send an electric generator to illumine the Shrine of the Báb. 'Abdu'l-Bahá was so pleased that He asked for three electric generators, and Little Brown Cat was so intrigued that she decided to watch very carefully to see what would happen next. Although three electric generators arrived in Haifa from America, nothing happened, which made Little Brown Cat curious. She was even more curious when an engineer arrived from America and 'Abdu'l-Bahá sent him home, telling him it wasn't time yet. And a little later, when a Persian engineer called Husayn[19] came all the way from India, 'Abdu'l-Bahá also told him that it wasn't the right time yet, but that when it was the right time he would be called to help.

Little Brown Cat watched and waited patiently from her favourite places in Haparsim Street, and just when she thought that nothing would ever happen, it did. It all began to get interesting one September day[20] when a young American arrived in Haparsim Street. His name was Curtis Kelsey, and he had been met at Haifa railway station by Fujita and a young man called Luṭfu'lláh Ḥakím in 'Abdu'l-Bahá's horse-drawn carriage, both of them waving and smiling at him as he stepped down from the train.[21]

Curtis, Fujita and Luṭfu'lláh shared a small bedroom in the Western Pilgrim House, and Little Brown Cat wondered how they would all fit in, because Fujita's suitcase was so large and so overflowing with his clothes that there wasn't much room for anything else. Little Brown Cat knew that Fujita liked to dress up in his special evening suit just for the fun of it, and she could hear Curtis laughing.

Work on the lighting of the Shrines of both the Báb and Bahá'u'lláh didn't begin immediately, and since Curtis loved to be busy, he spent his time looking for any jobs he could do while he was waiting. When he looked in the garage he found two cars[22] which hadn't been used for a while. As soon as he had them working again, he took 'Abdu'l-Bahá for drives up Mount Carmel, and Little Brown Cat was careful to keep well out of the way whenever Curtis drove one of the cars out of the garage.

Little Brown Cat suspected that the right time for installing the lighting might have finally arrived when Curtis started using the garage for sorting out lighting equipment and tools. Sometimes she crept inside to have a closer look when Curtis was busy, but she always made sure not to touch anything and to leave again when he was about to shut the garage doors.

As the work began, 'Abdu'l-Bahá told Curtis that he was to move between the Shrine of Bahá'u'lláh at Bahjí and the Shrine of the Báb in Haifa every two weeks, and although Little Brown Cat knew that she would miss her new friend when he was away at Bahjí, she reminded herself that bringing electric lighting to the Shrines was more important than her feelings. It was then that the Persian engineer, Husayn, returned to Haifa in order to help Curtis, but because they spoke different languages they found it quite difficult to talk to one another; Little Brown Cat noticed that at first they communicated by making facial expressions and signing with their hands, as they gradually began to share and understand words which they needed as they worked together.

Little Brown Cat was very happy when Curtis was working in Haifa, and so was Curtis, because it meant that he could spend precious time with 'Abdu'l-Bahá. Most days they had lunch together with Fujita in the Western Pilgrim House; 'Abdu'l-Bahá would tell them stories about the early Bahá'ís, and after the meal Curtis enjoyed the wonderful sense of peace as 'Abdu'l-Bahá gently pushed His turban back and sat quietly reading His letters. Sometimes after lunch Curtis and Fujita liked to play little tricks, and 'Abdu'l-Bahá enjoyed the opportunity to smile and laugh. Little Brown Cat liked it too, especially when she was involved and could join in the fun. Fujita always made sure that Little Brown Cat was hidden away in the kitchen during lunch, just so that he and Curtis could hear 'Abdu'l-Bahá ask them to open the door and let her out. As soon as the door was opened Little Brown Cat ran across to 'Abdu'l-Bahá, Who stroked her and gave her some food; Little Brown Cat was so happy to be close to 'Abdu'l-Bahá that as soon as she had finished eating she rubbed her head on His feet and purred loudly.[23]

Whilst Curtis and Husayn worked hard installing the electric lighting, visitors and pilgrims continued to come and go, and life seemed to carry on much as usual. There were times when Little Brown Cat thought that 'Abdu'l-Bahá looked quite tired as she watched Him walking to and from His home. But He never stopped His visits to the Western Pilgrim House or to the Shrine of the Báb, and Little Brown Cat had a secret wish that He never would, because she was so happy to know that He was close.

During the third week of November[24] as Little Brown Cat sat snoozing under the bougainvillea bush, she was suddenly aware of a new group of pilgrims arriving at the Western Pilgrim House, where 'Abdu'l-Bahá was standing ready to greet them. She thought she was used to all the different people who visited Haparsim Street, old and young, tall and short, noisy and quiet, from the east and the west, the north and the south. But when she caught sight of one of the new pilgrims from America she was so startled that she leapt to her four paws beneath the bougainvillea bush, her back arched and all the hairs on her tail fluffed out like a big brush.

There, standing in front of 'Abdu'l-Bahá, was the most alarming-looking man she had ever seen, or could ever have imagined. His name was Doctor Krug,[25] and his face was covered in scars from all the duels he had fought as a young man living in Germany. Little Brown Cat stared and stared as 'Abdu'l-Bahá greeted Dr. Krug with all the love He offered to everyone He met, and by the time they had walked through the gate to the Pilgrim House her arched back and fluffed-up tail had nearly returned to normal.

Not long after Little Brown Cat had settled back into her place under the bougainvillea bush she was surprised to see 'Abdu'l-Bahá walking across the road to His house with Dr. Krug and his wife. And she was even more surprised when she realised that 'Abdu'l-Bahá had invited them to stay in His own special room above the garage,[26] something she couldn't remember ever happening before. Little Brown Cat began to wonder what it was that was so special about Dr. Krug, because he was still the most alarming person she had ever seen.

Indeed, when Dr. Krug's wife had become a Bahá'í during 'Abdu'l-Bahá's visit to America,[27] he was so angry that he threw her Bahá'í books down the stairs; and it wasn't until 'Abdu'l-Bahá had lovingly asked him if he was happy that his heart had completely melted.

One dark night towards the end of November,[28] Little Brown Cat was awoken by someone running from 'Abdu'l-Bahá's house to the Western Pilgrim House, and she knew immediately that something had happened. Curtis, Fujita and Luṭfu'lláh Ḥakím ran from their little bedroom and across Haparsim Street, and had Little Brown Cat been able to follow them she would have seen them enter 'Abdu'l-Bahá's room, where He lay very, very still in His bed; and then she would have known what was so special about Dr. Krug, for at that very moment he was gently closing 'Abdu'l-Bahá's eyes.

'Abdu'l-Bahá had passed away peacefully, and as His family and local Bahá'ís started gathering outside His room Little Brown Cat crept quietly to her favourite spot beneath the bougainvillea bush. Not long afterwards she saw 'Abdu'l-Bahá's sister, the Greatest Holy Leaf, quietly and serenely moving amongst all the people gathered at the house and in the street, comforting them with kind words and gestures.

Little Brown Cat knew that although life would never be quite the same again, change was something which happens all the time, every day, every hour. She had seen change happening all around her, with different visitors, different weather, different smells and different sounds, and so she knew that it was just a question of accepting, even though she felt so sad.

The day following 'Abdu'l-Bahá's passing was a day which Little Brown Cat would never, ever, forget. Preparations had been made for His funeral,[29] and as daybreak dawned more and more people began arriving in Haparsim Street. When the funeral procession started its journey towards Mount Carmel, Little Brown Cat gazed out from the bougainvillea bush at all the people who had come to say goodbye to 'Abdu'l-Bahá; there were representatives from many different countries and religions, there were the rich and the poor, people who had known 'Abdu'l-Bahá and people who had loved Him from afar, and as they moved slowly through the streets of Haifa it became a vast procession of ten thousand people.

When Little Brown Cat eventually crept out from beneath the bougainvillea bush all was silent, but as she sat erect in the middle of the empty street she could hear the procession away in the far distance, slowly making its way up the slopes of Mount Carmel to the garden of the Shrine of the Báb, for it was there that 'Abdu'l-Bahá was to be laid to rest.

Little Brown Cat could only imagine what was happening, because she had never been to the Shrine of the Báb. Had she been present she would have seen all the people as they moved slowly up the hill from Haifa, 'Abdu'l-Bahá's casket[30] held high above their heads;

and she would have seen how, when they reached the
garden of the Shrine of the Báb, His casket was laid
very carefully on a table covered in a beautiful white
cloth as people from Muslim, Christian and Jewish
religions raised their voices in praise of 'Abdu'l-Bahá,
whom they all loved so much. And Little Brown Cat
would have watched in wonder as so many people from
so many different faiths seemed completely united as
they said their final goodbyes to 'Abdu'l-Bahá.

It was then that Little Brown Cat would have
seen how 'Abdu'l-Bahá's casket was lowered gently into
its resting place, close to that of The Báb. But because

Little Brown Cat wasn't there, she could only imagine what was happening, and as the day passed she found great comfort in knowing that she had been a part of 'Abdu'l-Bahá's funeral simply by sitting quietly in His garden in Haparsim Street.

In the days following 'Abdu'l-Bahá's passing His sister, the Greatest Holy Leaf, quietly took responsibility for ensuring that life for the Bahá'í's carried on as smoothly as possible. A few weeks later Little Brown Cat was greatly comforted when Shoghi Effendi returned from England,[31] and noticing how sad he was because his beloved Grandfather was no longer there, she tried to comfort him by rubbing her head gently against his feet.

As Little Brown Cat dozed and stretched under the bougainvillea bush or in 'Abdu'l-Bahá's garden, her secret hope was that life in Haparsim Street would return to normal, even though she knew in her heart that so much had already changed that returning to normal probably wasn't possible. And when, a few days after Shoghi Effendi's return, he discovered that he had been chosen to be Guardian of the Bahá'í Faith,[32] Little Brown Cat was comforted by the fact that, although life might be different for all the people she knew and loved, she still had her favourite places to walk and sleep in Haparsim Street, and she still had her friends Curtis and Fujita living close by in the Western Pilgrim House.

It was when Little Brown Cat was quietly walking behind Curtis one day that she began wondering about 'Abdu'l-Bahá's dearest wish to see Mount Carmel covered in light, shining across from the Shrine of the Báb to the Shrine of Bahá'u'lláh at Bahjí.

Since 'Abdu'l-Bahá's passing no work had taken place on the electric lighting, and just when Little Brown Cat was beginning to think that Shoghi Effendi and everyone else had forgotten all about it, she noticed that Curtis and Husayn had started working again.

Little Brown Cat hoped that with Shoghi

Effendi's return and work on the lighting continuing, there would be no more changes to worry about. Nevertheless, as she watched Shoghi Effendi coming and going from her spot under the bougainvillea bush, she noticed that he looked very tired, and she began to wonder if, in becoming the Guardian, he might need time to rest and prepare himself for the task. And of course, she was right, because just as Curtis and Husayn were finishing the lighting for the Shrines, Shoghi Effendi left Haifa for Switzerland.[33]

Little Brown Cat felt very very sad, because she loved Shoghi Effendi almost as much as she had loved 'Abdu'l-Bahá. And now that he had gone away she couldn't imagine how the Shrines of the Báb and Bahá'u'lláh would ever be bathed in light. But she needn't have worried, because Shoghi Effendi had left clear instructions that on the evening of April 20th, about two weeks after he left for Switzerland, all the lights would be lit.

Little Brown Cat knew that finally, after so much planning and hard work, 'Abdu'l-Bahá's wish was coming true. There was a great feeling of excitement that evening, spreading through the winding streets of Haifa and all the way up to the very top of Mount Carmel; and as the excitement grew Little Brown Cat decided to leave her favourite places in Haparsim Street and walk very slowly and carefully towards the

foot of Mount Carmel, to see for herself the miracle
of the electric lights. As darkness fell the Bahá'ís and
the people of Haifa stood in expectation, watching,
waiting, then marvelling when, at last, the light from
the Shrine of the Báb and the light from the Shrine of
Bahá'u'lláh met in a brilliant arc over the Bay of Haifa.

Never in her life had Little Brown Cat ventured as far as Carmel Avenue[34] and now, as she gazed up at the Shrine of the Báb for the very first time, she wallowed in the glorious light which poured down the mountain and along the Avenue, where excited children played and danced in their own shadows. And in that moment Little Brown Cat knew that, although 'Abdu'l-Bahá was no longer there in person, His love and His wise words would never go away.

It was with that thought that Little Brown Cat turned and began the long walk home. She was tired but happy as she finally arrived in Haparsim Street, where her dear friend Fujita had left her a small bowl of milk, a welcome treat before she settled herself for a lovely long sleep in the safety of 'Abdu'l-Bahá's garden.

# Notes

Throughout the story are links to the following notes, giving extra information or explanations where required; the bibliography lists all sources used.

1. Modern day Israel.
2. He moved to 7, Haparsim Street, which had been completed in 1908, and from 1910 it was His official residence. Following 'Abdu'l-Bahá's travels to the West, it became the place where pilgrims to the Baha'í World Centre were received.
3. The Báb was Bahá'u'lláh's predecessor, Who had been martyred in Shiraz in 1850.
4. *He Loved and Served, The story of Curtis Kelsey.* Nathan Rutstein. GR. Page 73.
5. Abu Sinan.
6. From the end of WW1 until mid-1920 Palestine was, in effect, being ruled by Britain. Haifa had been captured by British imperial troops in September 1918, and developing the harbour in Haifa was seen as being a primary objective of both the military and the civil administration of the city. Bugles, or in this case, bagpipes, were used to wake army personnel at sunrise.
7. Number 4, Haparsim.
8. *Bahá'u'lláh and the New Era*, eventually published in 1923.
9. 1919.

10. Cunningham V-3 motor car given by Mrs. Ella Goodall Cooper.

11. William Henry Randall with his wife Ruth and daughter Margaret (Bahíyyih) from Boston.

12. Known as an 'abā'.

13. 27<sup>th</sup> November 1919.

14. 27<sup>th</sup> November 1919.

15. In the spring of 1920 'Abdu'l-Bahá arranged for Shoghi Effendi to spend time convalescing at a sanatorium outside Paris before beginning his studies in Oxford.

16. 'Abdu'l-Bahá patting and feeding His cat is mentioned in *He Loved and Served*, page 74.

17. On 27<sup>th</sup> April 1920, Abdu'l-Bahá was given the title, Sir 'Abdu'l-Bahá Abbas, K.B.E at a ceremony in the garden of the Military Governor of Haifa. It was given to Him for the humanitarian work He undertook during the war. Although He accepted the honour as the gift of a 'just king', He never used the title.

18. Roy Wilhelm was a millionaire living in New York City who became a Bahá'í after a visit to 'Akká with his mother in 1907. He was posthumously named a Hand of the Cause by Shoghi Effendi.

19. Husayn-i-Kahrubayi.

20. 1921.

21. Luṭfu'lláh Ḥakím was a young man at the time he first lived in Haifa, where he helped Shoghi Effendi and also took care of the pilgrims. Much later, in 1951, he returned to Haifa at the request of Shoghi Effendi, who appointed him to the International Bahá'í Council. In 1963 he was elected onto the first Universal House of Justice.

22. The Cunningham which had arrived with Fujita, and a Ford.
23. This episode is mentioned in *He Loved and Served*, page 73.
24. 19<sup>th</sup> November 1921.
25. Dr. Krug was a very well-known and respected American surgeon.
26. 'Abdu'l-Bahá had recently had a small room built above the garage, accessible via a flight of outside stairs.
27. 1912.
28. 28<sup>th</sup> November 1921.
29. 29<sup>th</sup> November 1921.
30. Coffin.
31. He had been studying at Oxford University.
32. When 'Abdu'l-Bahá's Will and Testament was read out, Shoghi Effendi discovered that he had been chosen to be Guardian of the Bahá'í Faith, and that he was now responsible for guiding all the Bahá'ís in the world.
33. He left on April 5<sup>th</sup> 1922.
34. Now Ben Gurion Avenue.

# Bibliography

Nathan Rutstein. *He Loved and Served*
Oxford: George Ronald. 1982

Michael V Day. *Journey to a Mountain, Volume 1*
Oxford: George Ronald. 2017

Bahíyyih Winckler. *A Pilgrimage to Haifa 1919*
USA: Bahá'í Publishing Trust. 1996

Bahíyyih Winckler. *William Henry Randall. Disciple of 'Abdu'l-Bahá*
London: One World Publications. 1996

Shoghi Effendi & Lady Blomfield. *The Passing of 'Abdu'l-Bahá*
Haifa: Rosenfeld Bros. 1922

H.M. Balyuzi. *'Abdu'l-Bahá: The Centre of the Covenant of Bahá'u'lláh*
Oxford: George Ronald. 1971